T0085718

PILGRIM BELL

ALSO BY KAVEH AKBAR

POETRY

Calling a Wolf a Wolf

ANTHOLOGY

The Penguin Book of Spiritual Verse: 100 Poets on the Divine

PILGRIM BELL

POEMS

KAVEH AKBAR

Graywolf Press

This publication is made possible, in part, by the voters of Minnesota through a Minnesota State Arts Board Operating Support grant, thanks to a legislative appropriation from the arts and cultural heritage fund. Significant support has also been provided by Target Foundation, the McKnight Foundation, the Lannan Foundation, the Amazon Literary Partnership, and other generous contributions from foundations, corporations, and individuals. To these organizations and individuals we offer our heartfelt thanks.

MINNESOTA
STATE ARTS BOARD

CLEAN
WATER
LAND &
LEGACY
AMENDMENT

Published by Graywolf Press
250 Third Avenue North, Suite 600
Minneapolis, Minnesota 55401

www.graywolfpress.org

Published in the United States of America

ISBN 978-1-64445-059-8

2 4 6 8 9 7 5 3 1
First Graywolf Printing, 2021

Library of Congress Control Number: 2020944177

Cover painting and design: Hannah Bagshaw

CONTENTS

Any text that is not a holy text is an apostasy.

Then it is a holy text.

PILGRIM BELL

Dark on both sides.
Makes a window.
Into a mirror. A man.
Holds his palms out.
To gather dew.
Through the night. Uses it.
To wash before.
Dawn prayer.
Only a god.
Can turn himself into.
A god.
The earth buckles.
Almond trees bow.
To their own roots. Fear.
Comes only.
At our invitation but.
It comes. It came.

VINES

when I saw God
I trembled like a man I used the wrong pronouns

God bricked up my mouthhole
his fists were white as gold there were
roaches in my beard now I live like a widow

every day a heave of knitting patterns
and sex toys my family speaks of me

with such pride نوش تو روغنه they say
his bread is in oil I thank them for that and
for their chromosomes most of which

have been lovely I am lovely too my body
is hard and choked with juice like a plastic

throat stuffed with real grapes my turn-ons
include Rumi and fake leather my turn-
offs have all been ushered into the basement

I'll drink to them and to any
victory roaches in my beard I live now like a window

fat wet vines creep through onto my
floors in the pipes and through
the walls gentle as blue flames they curl

my living there is ice in my attic sugar on my
tile I am present and useless like a nose torn
from a face and set in a bowl

THE MIRACLE

Gabriel seizing the illiterate man, alone and fasting in a cave, and commanding READ, the man saying I can't, Gabriel squeezing him tighter, commanding READ, the man gasping I don't know how, Gabriel squeezing him so tight he couldn't breathe, squeezing out the air of protest, the air of doubt, crushing it out of his crushable human body, saying READ IN THE NAME OF YOUR LORD WHO CREATED YOU FROM A CLOT, and thus: literacy. Revelation.

It wasn't until Gabriel squeezed away what was empty in him that the Prophet could be filled with miracle. Imagine the emptiness in you, the vast cavities you have spent your life trying to fill—with fathers, mothers, lovers, language, drugs, money, art, praise—and imagine them gone. What's left? Whatever you aren't, which is what makes you—a house useful not because its floorboards or ceilings or walls, but because the empty space between them.

Gabriel isn't coming for you. If he did, would you call him Jibril, or Gabriel like you are here? Who is this even for?

One crisis at a time. Gabriel isn't coming for you. Cheese on a cracker, a bit of salty fish.

Somewhere a man is steering a robotic plane into murder. "Robot" from the Czech *robota*, meaning *forced labor*. Murder labor, forced. He never sees the bodies, which are implied by their absence. Like feathers on a paper bird.

Gabriel isn't coming for you. In the absence of cloud-parting, trumpet-blaring clarity, what? More living. More money, lazy sex. Mother, brother, lover. You travel and bring back silk scarves, a bag of chocolates for you-don't-know-who-yet. Someone will want them. Deliver them to an empty field. You fall asleep facing the freckle on your wrist.

Somewhere a woman presses a button that locks metal doors with people behind them. The locks are useful to her because there is an emptiness on the other side that holds the people's lives in place. She doesn't know the names of the people. Anonymity is an ancillary feature of the locks. "Ancillary," from the Latin *ancilla*, meaning *servant*. An emptiness to hold all their living.

You created from a clot: Gabriel isn't coming for you. You too full to eat. You too locked to door.

Too cruel to wonder.

Gabriel isn't coming. You too loved to love. Too speak to hear. Too wet to drink.

No Gabriel.

You too pride to weep. You too play to still. You too high to cum.

No. Gabriel won't be coming for you. Too fear to move. You too pebble to stone. Too saddle to horse. Too crime to pay. Gabriel, no. Not anymore. You too gone to save. Too bloodless to martyr. Too diamond to charcoal. Too nation to earth. You brute, cruel pebble. Gabriel. God of man. No. Cheese on a cracker. Mercy. Mercy.

GHAZAL FOR THE MEN I ONCE WAS

If you're immortal, God better be too. Otherwise? Otherwise. Hello, have you
disrobed? The nursemaid is stomping her hooves. Don't make her fret like that.

Dip a finger in your bourbon, tap it to your lip. Bad water. Bedwetter. Now watch
these hands through your blood—jealous moths. How do they heaven, upset like that?

The hungry bear won't dance. Bad milk burnt her tongue. How to find your voice:
try. You're bound to it like a knight to his century. Everything forgets like that.

The key, filed smooth to fit every lock, opens none. The bitter mourning
uselessly in the rain. In the beginning was the eye, and the eye was wet like that.

Like a pin pushed through a pane of glass. Like life lasting longer than you
can bear. Like a sundial gone bad. Like your own name. Dead set like that.

REZA'S RESTAURANT, CHICAGO, 1997

the waiters milled about filling sumac
         shakers clearing away
plates of onion and radish
my father pointed to each person whispered
Persian about the old man with the silver
         beard whispered *Arab* about the woman with
the eye mole *Persian* the teenager pouring
water *White* the man on the phone
                I was eight
still soft as a thumb and amazed
I asked how he could possibly tell when
              they were all brown-
skin-dark-haired like us almost everyone
         in the restaurant looked like us
           he smiled a proud
      little smile a warm nest
of lip said *it's easy* said *we're just uglier*

        he returned to his lamb but I was baffled hardly
touched my gheimeh I had big glasses and bad
      teeth I felt plenty Persian
               when the woman
        with light eyes and blonde-brown
hair left our check my father looked at me
      I said *Arab?* he shook his head laughed
        we drove home I grew up it took years to
      put together what my father
meant that day my father who listened
      exclusively to the Rolling Stones
who called the Beatles
         a band for girls
      my father who wore only black even
        around the house whose umbrella
      made it rain whose arms could
            cut chicken wire and make stew and
      bulged with old farm scars my father my

father my father built
the world the first sound I ever heard
was his voice whispering the azan
in my right ear I didn't need anything
else my father cherished
that we were ugly and so being ugly
was blessed I smiled with all my teeth

THERE ARE 7,000 LIVING LANGUAGES

Here is one:

Try to be more than merely good

Here is another:

تلاش ناکافی است

Of the others, I know mostly
cuisine—soufflé, berbere, tamale.

☐

It's delicious
being so governed

by the primacy
of my tongue.

☐

Snips
and snails.

☐

There was an empty jar of olive oil
labeled پول برای پسران فقیر

We filled it up with coins.
Money for poor boys.

☐

Needles and pins.
Needles and pins.

When a boy starts speaking
his trouble begins.

☐

Lifting my skirt to the new day—

☐

The deviators

follow the poets.
See them wander

in the valley,
saying that which they do not?

☐

My car doesn't hit the car,

the two cars *collide*.

☐

Miserable islands.
Tinker, tailor.

There is something terrible
beneath all I am able to say.

☐

Needle-back wasp

sleeping under my tongue:

I weave,
we weave.

□

The tapestries either fall apart
or they don't.

THE VALUE OF FEAR

is in its sound, sewing song
to throat. The pale thrush

trills the snow while a lonely brute
hides in a fist of crickets,

hiding in the sound
under the floorboards is a brute, dizzy
with sound.

☐

To build a raft of the dead
you have to tie them together

by their hair, and even then
it won't be

crickets, it won't be a good raft.
So much of escape is
luck, a magnetic

north, sound
sewing silence to
each tiny muscle of the neck.

☐

The value of joy fades when you
notice an uncle

marching an uncle marching an uncle
out a picture frame.

So you let
a child-thief's hand in your pocket

because you see her
      skin is badly scarred. The value

of joy is in its
      asking, *what now shall I repair?* Dizzy

      joy, dizzy is the soul,
dizzy is the soul with all its lies

      about the soul.

MOTHERS I ONCE WAS

Mother fingers in the mud. Mother begging bowl.
Mother lace-weaver drumming her web, babies
eating her whole. Bleachable mother. Mother apron
smeared with flour. Mother flower. Mother Florida,

the wet bone. The marble throne. Mother sent back.
Mother bent back curling like script. Mother depended
on light. Mother? Depends on the night.

Mother for whom the whole sky.

Mother hiding in the curtains, humming too loud.
Maggot mother at the shroud. Mother thought it possible.
Mother was wrong. Mothersong. Our Lady Mother of Wet Beds

and Aggressive Disgrace. Mother persimmon, name sounds
the way she tastes. Mother with all of creation fattening.
Mother who held on while it was happening.

PILGRIM BELL

My savior has powers and he needs.
To be convinced to use them.
Up until now he has been.
A no-call no-show. Curious menace.
Like a hornet's nest buzzing.
On a plane wing. Savior. Younger than.
I pretend to be. Almost everyone is.
Younger than I pretend to be. I am a threat.
Even in my joy. Like a cat who. Playing kills.
A mouse and tongues.
It back to life. The cat lives.
Somewhere between wonder.
And shame. I live in a great mosque.
Built on top of a flagpole.
Whatever happens happens.
Loudly. All day I hammer the distance.
Between earth and me.
Into faith. Blue light pulls in through.
The long crack in my wall. Braids.
Into a net. The difference between.
A real voice and the other kind.
The way its air vibrates.
Through you. The way air.
Vibrates. The violence.
In your middle ear.

I WOULDN'T EVEN KNOW WHAT TO DO WITH A THIRD CHANCE

What's inside my body is more or less the same
as what's inside yours—here, the river girl clutching her toy whistle.
Here, the black snake covered in scabs. Follow my neckline,

the beginning will start beginning again. I swear on my
head and eyes, there are moments in every day when
if you asked me to leave, I would. Head and eyes. Heaven

is all preposition—above, among, around, within—and if you must,
you can live any place that's a place. A failure of courage is still
a victory for safety. Bravery pitches its refugee tent

at the base of my brain and slowly starves, chipping into
darkness like a clay bird bouncing down a well. All night
I eat garlic cream, water my dead orchids.

In what world does any of it seem credible?
God's word is a melody, and melody requires repetition.
God's word is a melody I sang once then forgot.

Unable to sleep, or pray, I stand

ROBERT HAYDEN

PILGRIM BELL

The stillness you prize.
Won't prize you back. Two beefsteaks.
Ripening on a windowsill.
A purple tray.
Piled with coal.

Become the many-roomed house.
You walk through in dreams. Show me.
On the great blue door.
Where it hurts.

This is the season where grace.
Is the likeliest. Where the uttermost.
Angels weigh down our galaxy.
With sound. A silver ring.
Lost in the bedsheets is still.

A silver ring. You can either be.
More holy or more full but.

Not both. See how the hot.
Element glows red. How.
Honey cools the tea. Suppose.
There was a reason for it.
Suppose there wasn't.

MY EMPIRE

My empire made me
happy because it was an empire
and mine.

I was too stupid to rage at anything.

Babies cried at birth, it was said,
because the devil pricked them as introduction
to knowledge.

I sat fingering my gilded frame, counting
grievances like toes:

here my mother, here my ring,
here my sex, and here my king.

All still there. Wrath is the desire
to repay what you've suffered.

Kneeling on coins
before the minor deity in the mirror.
Clueless as a pearl.

That the prophets arrived not to ease our suffering
but to experience it seems—can I say this?—
a waste?

My empire made me happy
so I loved, easily, its citizens—such loving
a kind of birth, an introduction to pain.

Whatever I learn makes me angry to have learned it.

The new missiles can detect a fly's heartbeat
atop a pile of rubble from 6,000 miles away.
That flies have hearts, 104 cells big, that beat.

And because of this knowing:
a pile of rubble.

The prophets came to participate in suffering
as if to an amusement park, which makes
our suffering the main attraction.

In our brochure:
a father's grief over his dead father,
the thorn broken off in a hand.

My empire made me happy
because it was an empire, cruel,

and the suffering wasn't my own.

IN THE LANGUAGE OF MAMMON

Behold the poet, God's
incarnate spit in the mud,
chirping like lice in a fire.
Songs to stir the arousable horn.
Songs to make money
which he treats like food:
fit as much as you can
in your mouth, never shit.

His most intoxicating delusion—
that evil might be soluble in art.

History, butcher.
Da mihi castitatem et continentiam,
sed noli modo.

Don't judge him
by the first thought to enter his head.
Judge him by the second.

MY FATHER'S ACCENT

A boy, prettier than me, who loved me because
my vocabulary and because my orange pills, once asked me
to translate my father's English.

☐

This poem wants me to translate it too.
Idiot poem, idiot hands for writing it:

an accent isn't sound.
Only those to whom it seems alien
would flatten an accent to sound.

☐

My poem grew up here, sitting in this American chair
staring out at this lifeless American snow.

Black grass dying up out of this snow,
through a rabbit's

long tracks, like a ghost
sitting upright
saying *oh*.

☐

But even that's a lie.

No tracks.
Just black grass, blue snow.
I can't write this

without trying to make it
beautiful. Submission, resistance, surrender.

☐

On first
inspecting Adam, the devil entered his lips.

Watch: the devil enters Adam's lips,
crawls through his throat, through his guts
to finally emerge out his anus.

He's all hollow! the devil giggles.
He knows his job will be easy, a human just one long
desperation to be filled.

□

My father's white undershirt peeking out
through his collar. My father's hand slicing skin, gristle,
from a chicken carcass I hold still against the cutting board.

Sometimes he bites his bottom lip to suppress
what must be
rage. It must be rage

because it makes no sound. My vast
terror at what I can't hear,

at my ignorance, is untranslatable.
My father speaks in perfect English.

THERE IS NO SUCH THING AS AN ACCIDENT OF THE SPIRIT

You can cut the body in half
like a candle to double its light
but you need to prepare yourself
for certain consequences.
All I know about science—
neurons, neutrinos, communicable
disease—could fit inside
a toothpick, with wood to spare.
Blow it away, like an eyelash or
lamplight. Show me one beast
that loves itself as relentlessly
as even the most miserable man.
I'll wait. Verily, they sent down
language, filling us with words
like seawater filling a lung. You
can hear them listening now
for our listening. Ask me again
about my doubt—turquoise
today and almond-hard. It speaks
only of what it can't see itself:
one chromosome bowing politely
to the next, or the way our lips still
sometimes move when we sleep.

FORFEITING MY MYSTIQUE

It is pretty to be sweet
and full of pardon like
a flower perfuming the
hands that shred it, but
all piety leads to a single
point: the same paradise
where dead lab rats go.

If you live small you'll
be resurrected with the
small, a whole planet
of minor gods simpering
in the weeds. I don't know
anyone who would kill
anyone for me. As boys

my brother and I
would play love, me
drawing stars on
the soles of his feet,
him tickling my back.
Then we'd play harm,
him cataloging my sins

to the air, me throwing
him into furniture.
The algorithms for living
have always been
delicious and hollow,
like a beetle husk in a
spider's paw. Hafez said

fear is the cheapest room
in a house, that we ought
to live in better
conditions. I would

happily trade all my
knowing for plusher
carpet, higher ceilings.

Some nights I force
my brain to dream me
Persian by listening
to old home movies
as I fall asleep. In the
mornings I open my eyes
and spoil the séance. Am I

forfeiting my mystique?
All bodies become sicker
bodies—a kind of object
permanence, a curse bent
around our scalps resembling
grace only at the tattered
edges. It's so unsettling

to feel anything but good.
I wish I was only as cruel as
the first time I noticed
I was cruel, waving my tiny
shadow over a pond to scare
the copper minnows.
Rockabye, now I lay me

down, etcetera. The world
is what accumulates—
the mouth full of meat,
the earth full of dust.
My grandfather
taught his parrot
the ninety-nine holy

names of God. Al-Muzil:
The Humiliator. Al-Waarith:

The Heir. Once, after
my grandfather had been
dead a year, I woke
from a dream (I was a
sultan guzzling milk

from a crystal boot) with
his walking cane deep in
my mouth. I kept sucking until
I fell back asleep. Al-Muhsi:
The Numberer. There are only
two bones in the throat, and that's
if you count the clavicle. This

seems unsafe, overdelicate,
like I ought to ask for
a third. As if anyone
living would offer.
Corporeal friends are
spiritual enemies, said
Blake, probably gardening

in the nude. Today I'm trying
to scowl more, mismatch
my lingerie. Nobody
seems bothered enough.
Some saints spent their
whole childhoods biting
their teachers' hands and

sprinkling salt into spider-
webs, only to be redeemed
by a fluke shock
of grace just before
death. May I feather
into such a swan soon.
The Book of Things

Not to Touch gets longer
every day: on one
page, the handsome puppy
bred only for service. On
the next, my mother's
face. It's not even enough
to keep my hands to myself—

there's a whole chapter
about the parts of me
that could get me
into trouble. In Farsi,
we say jaya shomah khallee
when a beloved is absent
from our table—literally:

your place is empty. I don't
know why I waste my time
with the imprecision of saying
anything else, like using
a hacksaw to slice a strawberry
when I have a razor in my
pocket. A slice of straw-

berry so fresh it shudders.
One immortal soul spoils
the average for everyone,
reminds us the whole game
is rigged. This is a fact,
but barely. Which is to say
it is.

COTTON CANDY

To go to heaven, we make heaven come to us.—JOHN DONNE

yes John I tried that the results were
underwhelming my liver practically
    leapt out of my body my mother
wept nightly for eight years
            my living
    curled its hands around her throat
not choking exactly but like the squeeze
of an outgrown collar
          in Iran
    she spoke my father's language with
such a thick accent his family laughed when she
talked but she still talked and she listened diligent
    as a holy sword
        the reward
      for goodness
    is just more goodness and sometimes
not even that once I allowed a beetle to
        scuttle back under my fridge in a week
    she became a thousand beetles I packed
my bags and left for good the apartment
was hers
    a mother
      is someone who
    is looking to improve
          mine was
a climbable trellis her nation-
    flag was a leather apron fastened
    to a spear
        if I were a mother
I'd lose my child at the fair and go on
riding rides zooming through the
    air singing *Which way I fly is*
      heaven! I myself am heaven! But

my mother hated rides
she was happy to buy me cotton candy and
sit on a bench
smiling
she'd watch me eat the whole bag

AGAINST THE PARTS OF ME THAT THINK THEY KNOW ANYTHING

They want to put out the light of God with their mouths—
want, like the sovereignty of the dead, extending just short of flesh. Their
today is broken, they suggest *tomorrow*, who right now is dancing in the sun with
putty over his eyes. Like an ocean coughing up trash, I'm squeezing God
out from my pores, intention throbbing like a moon. Which of
the jokes I told was best—the difference between man and light?
Light won't ask for your tongue. Good joke, the taste of lemon. The
official death toll rising while we sleep. It's crude how they've figured out
God, tacky as jugglers at a funeral. Just let me grieve what I've lost. They were put
with me fully built, passionless as shoelaces, pitying even my name. To
their credit, they weren't given what I have: majesty and the heft of a face. They want
mouths like mine that can blow out tiny fires. The mercy of speech. Of sleep. Of they.

PILGRIM BELL

How long can you speak.
Without inhaling. How long.
Can you inhale without.
Bursting apart. History is wagging.
Its ass at us. Twirling in its silver.
Cape. I want to kiss.
Your gloves. I want you to kiss.
My friends. Can you see the wet.
Azalea quivering.
On its vine. Its ripening.
Dread. If it never rained again.
I would still wear.
My coat. Still wrap.
My socks in plastic. Doing.
One thing is a way.
Of not doing.
Everything else.
Today I answer only.
To my war name. Wise.
Salt. I can make.
A stone float off into.
The sky. I can make.
A whole family.
Disappear. I know.
So many people.
Have been awful to you.
I've given each one.
A number. When you're ready.
I will ask you to draw me.
Their hands.

SEVEN YEARS SOBER

Trust God but tie your camel. Trust
God. The bottle by the bed the first

few weeks. Just in case. Trust.

After the nights of too-relaxed-to-
breathe. After the nights—no repetition,

only insistence. Trust.

Buying raspberries to
watch them rot. Dipping bread in water.

Trust. You find a gold tooth washed up
on the beach. So long in coming. Gurfa:

the volume of water that can fit
in your hand.

Trust God.
The volume of your hand.

But carry water.

You know of the how, but I know of the how-less.
RABIʿA AL-BASRI

A pilgrim is a person who is up to something.
ANNE CARSON

PILGRIM BELL

I demand.
To be forgiven.

I demand.
A sturdier soul.

Every person I've ever met.
Has been small enough.

To fit.
In my eye.

AN OVERSIGHT

I murdered my least defensible vices,

stacking them like bodies

in the surf. An armada of nurses rode in

to cherish the dead: *Try harder, little*

moons, they said to the corpses. Winter

followed winter. Horses coughed

blood into the sand. Some pain

stays so long its absence becomes

a different pain—

                    They say it's not

faith if you can hold it in your hands

but I suspect the opposite may be true,

that real faith passes first through the body

like an arrow. Consider our whole galaxy

staked in place by a single star. I fear

we haven't said nearly enough about that.

ULTRASOUND

my father is tying concertina
wire around his garden
now all but ruined by
squirrels deer and worst
of all rabbits with cucumber
seeds stuck to their
tails   I am an apex predator my father is
an apex predator God makes
us in pairs   my mother searches the lawn

☐

for four-leaf clovers pinning them
to a scrapbook my mother pinning
moments to time she gives each one
a name Buck Comes onto Porch and
Hospital Note from Kaveh   while
she makes tea inside I search
the house for a lighter and can't
even find matches   my mother hovers in
the kitchen like a strange tune

☐

in the tune my mother is out
of saffron and has no money
for more   she weeps over her
bleach-white rice until my
father comes in cracks an egg
over the plate bursts
the yolk says *see* says *yellow*   my mother
smiles so big and sad she wrinkles into
the future where

☐

                    my eyes
are yellow again maybe from the yolk
maybe something else   my fur is coming in
so thick my mother would squeal
with pride if she could see it   when she
was pregnant I kicked so hard so
often she could barely
sleep   staying up all
night she thought she must
be full of bunnies

PALACE MOSQUE, FROZEN

the heart is a muscle as stupid

as a hamstring or a miniature

bright   dust

as we say them   pillowed floor

we see our prayers

iris with its ridiculous blossoms

blooming only through ice

Tucked away in our tiny bedroom so near each other
the edge of my prayer rug covered the edge of his, my
brother and I prayed. We were 18 and 11 maybe, or 19
and 12. He was back from college where he built his own
computer and girls kissed him on the mouth. I was barely
anything, just wanted to be left alone to read and watch
The Simpsons.

We prayed together as we had done thousands of times,
rushing ablutions over the sink, laying our janamazes out
toward the window facing the elm which one summer
held an actual crow's nest full of baby crows: fuzzy, black-
beaked fruit, they were miracles we did not think to
treasure.

My brother and I hurried through sloppy postures of
praise, quiet as the light pooling around us. The room
was so small our twin bed took up nearly all of it, and
as my brother, tall and endless, moved to kneel, his foot
caught the coiled brass doorstop, which issued forth a
loud *brooong*. The noise crashed around the room like a
long, wet bullet shredding through porcelain.

My brother bit back a smirk and I tried to stifle a snort
but solemnity ignored our pleas—we erupted, laughter
quaking out our faces into our bodies and through the
floor. We were hopeless, laughing at our laughing, our
glee an infinite rope fraying off in every direction.

It's not that we forgot God or the martyrs or the Prophet's
holy word—quite the opposite, in fact, we were boys built
to love what was right in front of our faces: my brother
and I draped across each other, laughing tears into our
prayer rugs.

HOW TO SAY THE IMPOSSIBLE THING

Plainly. The man's teeth so clean
they had to be fake. My piss

still hardened into Bernadette's carpet.
To say it plainly

that I don't trust myself?
And that I never will?

When I say "myself"
I mean: obviousness

ruins things—fire,
vodka, morphine, soap.

Thy hands thy sky thy chalice

SHADIAN INCIDENT

In 1975, the People's Liberation Army attacked the city of Shadian, home to China's largest population of Hui Muslims. One thousand Hui were killed and more than four thousand homes were destroyed.

I knew them when they were just
geraniums when they
were still blood-pink ears in a pulsing
womb

     grief requires
only a tongue and a crown ask
anyone ask a bell
       it'll answer in
three slow wails

        the mosque
loudspeaker groans down to the
children or at least down to
their beds empty today and
perfectly

       the soldiers pawned
their guns for cigarettes
soupbones model
trains   there is dust
where there should
have been men   air
where there
should have been
men   they forced him
to wear a pig's head
around his neck
        action
will be judged according
to intention
      they forced
him to wear a pig's
head around his neck

DESPITE MY EFFORTS EVEN MY PRAYERS HAVE TURNED INTO THREATS

Holy father I can't pretend
I'm not afraid to see you again
but when the time comes
I believe my courage
will expand like a sponge
cowboy in water. My earth-
father came to America knowing
no English save Rolling Stones
lyrics and how to say *thanks
God*. Will his goodness roll
over to my tab and if yes, how
soon? I'm sorry for neglecting
your myriad signs, obvious
now as a hawk's head
on an empty plate. I keep
nearly waking up to whatever
I miss most: whiskey-
glass, pill bottles, my mother's
oleander—sweet and
evergreen but toxic in all
its parts. I know it's silly
to keep what I've kept from you,
you always so charmed
by my weakness. I just
imagine you fed up with
all your making, like a virtuoso
trying not to smash apart her
flute onstage. Plus, my sins
were practically devotional:
two peaches stolen from
a bodega, so sweet I savored
even what I flossed from
my teeth. I know it's no excuse,
but even now I'm drooling. Consider
the night I spent reading

another man's lover *The Dream
Songs* in bed—we made it to
"a green living / drops
limply" before we were
tangled into each other, cat
still sleeping at our feet. Allow
me these treasures, Lord.
Time will break what doesn't
bend—even time. Even you.

ESCAPE TO THE PALACE

it's beautiful to
breathe drugs
off a house key or
through a glass bird
but the last thing I
remember was
quietly eating all
of mine in an air-
port bathroom my
pockets were full of
orange slices they
were soaking
through my pants
grace sent a note
that said *prepare*
your interior
I will be arriving
at dawn I read it
on the toilet
I am trying to
be as honest
as possible
the door was
locked the faucet
was leaking
I nearly missed
my flight

GHAZAL FOR A NATIONAL EMERGENCY

Look: people leaping off ladders, landing in Washington.
Curses lift like smoke from throats warm the air in Washington.

A man selling water on a median sweats into his eyes. The cars blur
into a string of silver anchors, pinning the world to Washington.

Loss is a vector, all magnitude and direction: computers detect a pear
rotting under Damascus rubble from all the way in Washington.

Lives pile up like constellations, diamonds on black silk ready to be
set in God's crown. Fetch Him, and bring Him back to Washington.

Tulip trees crack in the heat, then shatter into crosses, paper
pulp. Embrace your rage and this will be easier, winks Washington.

Satan is a long bone shucked hard from the mouth that grew him,
a great elephant tusk shooting up out the grave of Washington.

The dead want too much. To scare the living, they gasp their old names—
the living panic, plug their ears, and send their dread to Washington.

READING FARROKHZAD IN A PANDEMIC

The title is a lie;
I can't read Farsi.

ما هر چه را که باید از دست داده باشیم از دست داده ایم

I can make out:

"we lose,
we lose."

I type it into a translation app:
"we have lost everything we need to lose."

In between what I read and what is written:
"need," "everything."

☐

Here, the waving flag.
Here, the other world.

Because we need mail, people die.

☐

Because we need groceries, people die.

I write "*we* need"
knowing *we* dilutes

☐

my responsibility,
like watercolors dipped

in a fast river.
Get behind me, English.

☐

When I text
ما هر چه را که باید از دست داده باشیم از دست داده ایم

to my dad he writes back,
"we have lost whatever we had to lose."

Hammering
pentameter.

Whatever we
had.

People die because they look like him.
My uncle jailed, his daughter killed.

☐

This a real fact too wretched for
letters. And yet:

My uncle jailed.

☐

His daughter killed.

Waving world,
the other flag—

there is room in the language for being
without language.

☐

So much of *wet* is *cold*.
So much of *diamond* is *light*.

☐

I want both my countries
to be right

to fear me.

We have lost
whatever

we had to lose.

FAMOUS AMERICANS AND WHY THEY WERE WRONG

A ribbon around an oak tree reads
Brother. The oak's roots

sinking deeper into the dirt.
A heart

can sink too, like a root, or a library
whose architect forgot

to factor in the weight of its books. First you lose
Romance, then

Fiction, History. At the center of a heart
is data, the same

idiot degradation that turned the stars
into us. I hope somebody

forgets you today too. I hope somebody cuts
that ribbon free.

PILGRIM BELL

The self I am today.
Involves me.
As a lake. Involves.
Its cattails.
It bears me.
Tolerates.
My cotton.

I would prefer.
Not. To be outlived.
By anyone.

I reserve the right.
To refuse. Enchantment.

The fables I tell.
Always end. Wrong.
The good archer.
Dead.
By a stream.

By a stream.
The villains.
Counting.
Their gold.

I am so vulnerable.
To visionaries.
And absolute.
Certainty.

Tell me how to live.
And I will live that way.

AGAINST MEMORY

it may have been   courage

how I banished
my own knowing

dropped it
             like a book burning in my hands

                    it grows   somewhere

                         a circle of thistle seed
                         sprouting beneath the feeder

                              I envied   the wicked when I saw
                         the prosperity
                                   of the wicked

                                   I needed
                    fewer moving parts

                         an hourglass
             has thousands

                              a sundial has only

                                   the earth

haven't I always been happiest
      when a little simple

                                   when sad and too sleepy

                                        to speak

all of language   began

       with a single

           sound

O—

      no

   no

            it was

the
   O

     the

     hour

it
   was

Al-Harith bin Hisham asked the Prophet,
"O God's Messenger! How is the Divine Inspiration revealed to you?"

The Prophet replied,
"Sometimes it is revealed like the ringing of a bell."

HADITH 4:438

THE PALACE

It's hard to remember who I'm talking to
    and why. The palace burns, the palace
is fire
    and my throne is comfy and
square.

□

Remember: the old king invited his subjects into his home
to feast on stores of apple tarts and sweet lamb.

        To feast on sweet lamb of stories.
He believed

they loved him, that his goodness
had earned him their goodness.

Their goodness dragged him into the street
and tore off

his arms, plucked
        his goodness out, plucked his fingers out
                like feathers.

□

There are no good kings.
Only beautiful palaces.

□

Who here could claim to be merely guilty?
        The mere.

        My life
growing monstrous
with ease.

To be an American my father left his siblings
                believing
he'd never see them again. My father
                wanted to be Mick Jagger. My father
        went full ghost,
ended up working on duck farms for thirty years. Once a sleep,
        a couch,
        he coughed up a feather.

                ☐

        America could be a metaphor, but it isn't.
        Asleep on the couch, he coughed up a white duck feather.

                ☐

There are no doors in America.
Only king-sized holes.

                ☐

To be an American is to be a scholar
of opportunity.

Opportunity costs.

Every orange I eat disappears the million
peaches, plums, pears I could have eaten

but didn't.

In heaven, opportunity costs.
In her heaven

my mother grows
peaches, plums, pears, and I eat them till I pass out

and wake up in heaven—

wake up, and eat some more. I couldn't dream of doing anything
by halves. Whatever it is, I'll take the whole
                                        bouquet. Please and soon.

☐

Are you still listening?
        Every person I touch
                costs me ten million I'll never meet. Persons and persons,

        inside each
        a palace on fire. Inside each

Mick Jagger wearing a gorilla-pelt coat covered in ostrich feathers.
He calls it *glamouflage*.

☐

What's gone, but still seen?

☐

Luckless soldiers,
the pencil pushed slowly through my brother's tricep.

(What's gone, but still seen?)

He didn't scream, just let his eyes water.
If I smile even a little: they start sharpening their swords.

And they're right. This is no time for joy.
This is no time. The palace burns.
Pencil pushes slowly through my brother's brother.

(What's still, but seen gone?)

□

A king governs best
in the dark, where you can't see his hands move. A king

doesn't see us
watching the king.

We sew God's initials into our workshirts

while our babies get thinner.
The babies do not see us

watching our babies
get thinner.

Our babies born addicted to fear of babies.
Our babies gumming apples in the sun.

□

America? the broken headstone.
America? far enough away from itself.

□

Hello, this is Kaveh speaking:
I wanted to be Keats
(but I've already lived six years too long).

Hello, this is Keats speaking:
it is absurd to say anything now
(much less anything new).

Hello, this is no one speaking:
hibiscus bloom, wet feathers
(a tiny thumb of ash).

□

To be American is to be a hunter.

To be American. Who can be American?

To be American is to be? What? A hunter? A hunter
who shoots only money.
            No, not money—
            money.

☐

I have a kitchen device
that lets me spin lettuce.

There is no elegant way
        to say this—people
        with living hearts
        that could fit in my chest
want to melt the city where I was born.

At his elementary school in an American suburb,
a boy's shirt says: "We Did It to Hiroshima, We Can Do It to Tehran!"

☐

At his elementary school in an American suburb,
a boy's shirt says: "We Did It to Hiroshima, We Can Do It to Tehran!"

☐

A boy's shirt says: "We Did It to Hiroshima, We Can Do It to Tehran!"

He is asked to turn his shirt inside out.
He is asked? His insides, out.
After he complies, his parents sue the school district.

Our souls want to know
how they were made,
            what is owed.

These parents want their boy
to want to melt my family,
and I live among them.

Palace throne. Comfy, burning.
I draw it without lifting my pen.
I draw it fat as creation—

       empty as a footprint.

☐

How to live? reading poems, breathing shallow,
spinning lettuce.

☐

America the shallow breath,
how to live?

The shallow trap, America
catching

only what is too small to eat.

☐

The dead keep warm under America
while my mother fries eggplant on a stove.

☐

I am not there.
I am elsewhere in America (I am always
elsewhere in America) writing this, writing this, writing this, English
is my mother's first language,
but not mine.

I might have said bademjan.
I might have said khodafez.

     Sizzling oil, great fists of smoke, writing this.

☐

The first insect drawn by man was a locust.
Art is where what we survive survives.

Sizzling oil, great fists of smoke. Art. Sizzling oil.
My mother fries eggplant. The first

insect drawn by man survives.

☐

Who to kiss the prom queen?
     Brain pulsing like an oyster.

Who to win the war?
America rises

        covered in
the tiny grains of its own making:

fresh bread pocked with flour dust.

Mistyping in an email I write,
I lose you so much today,

then leave it.

Forbidden mercies, water bowl held
to a prisoner's lips,

     windmills spinning around
like drunk teenagers.

◻

Any document of civilization is also a document of barbarism
      says the palace, burning.

            I, a man,
            am what I do not say.

America, I warn you, if you invite me into your home
I will linger,

            kissing my beloveds frankly,
                  pulling up radishes
                  and capping all your pens.

            There are no good kings,
      only burning palaces.

      Lose me today, so much.

NOTES

"The Miracle" owes a debt of gratitude to Daschielle Louis.

"There Are 7,000 Living Languages" adapts lines from "And the poets? The deviators follow them" in Ash-Shu'ara 26:224.

The epigraph "Unable to sleep, or pray, I stand" is the opening line of Robert Hayden's "Ice Storm."

"My Empire" paraphrases a moment from Seneca's *De Ira* in which he quotes Aristotle saying wrath is the "desire to repay the evil one has suffered."

"In the Language of Mammon" owes debts of gratitude to Kamau Braithwaite's typographical innovations, Marwa Helal's "Arabic" form, and the elegance of written RTL languages such as Farsi and Arabic. "Da mihi castitatem et continentiam, sed noli modo" is from Augustine: "Grant me chastity and continence, but not yet."

"Forfeiting My Mystique" responds to an image ("the flower that gives its fragrance to even the hand that crushes it") traditionally attributed to the son-in-law of the Prophet, Hazrat Ali, though it doesn't appear in his book of sermons, *Nahjul Balagha*. The Hafez excerpt is taken from a poem translated by Daniel Ladinsky under the title, "Your Mother and My Mother." The William Blake excerpt is paraphrased from his letter to Thomas Butts of April 25, 1803.

"Cotton Candy" takes its epigraph from John Donne's "Funeral Elegies." The italicized portion plays on a line from John Milton's *Paradise Lost*.

"Against the Parts of Me That Think They Know Anything" is a kind of Golden Shovel, a form invented by Terrance Hayes paying homage to Gwendolyn Brooks. This poem features a line from the Quran, As-Saff 61:8, "They want to put out the light of God with their mouths," running down the left margin and up the right.

"Seven Years Sober" paraphrases a moment ("there can be no repetition because the essence of that expression is insistence") from Gertrude Stein's "Portraits and Repetition." "Trust God but tie your camel" is a quote attributed to the Prophet Muhammad.

The epigraph "You know of the how, but I know of the how-less" is from Rabi'a al-Basri, an eighth-century Sufi mystic. She is sometimes referred to as Rabi'a al-'Adawiyya al-Qaysiyya, or simply as Rabi'a.

The epigraph "A pilgrim is a person who is up to something" is from Anne Carson's *Plainwater.*

"Shadian Incident" recalls historical atrocities deserving of further reading; Alice Su's "Harmony and Martyrdom among China's Hui Muslims" is a stirring primer.

"Despite My Efforts Even My Prayers Have Turned into Threats" quotes from John Berryman's "Dream Song 19."

"Against Memory" plays on a phrase from Psalm 73:3.

"The Palace" is for Ilya Kaminsky, and contains an italicized paraphrase of a moment ("There is no document of civilization which is not at the same time a document of barbarism") from Walter Benjamin's "On the Concept of History."

ACKNOWLEDGMENTS

Deep, abiding gratitude to the editors of the publications where these poems first appeared, often in earlier versions and/or under different titles:

The Academy of American Poets' *Poem-A-Day*: "Ultrasound," "My Father's Accent"
The Atlantic: "Against the Parts of Me That Think They Know Anything"
Blackbird: "Against Memory"
BuzzFeed: "Cotton Candy"
The Georgia Review: "Palace Mosque, Frozen"
Granta: "How Prayer Works"
Literary Hub: "Reading Farrokhzad in a Pandemic"
Los Angeles Review of Books: "Pilgrim Bell (Dark on both sides)"
The Nation: "Pilgrim Bell (My savior has powers)"
New England Review: "The Value of Fear"
The New Yorker: "The Palace," "My Empire"
Nowruz Journal: "There Is No Such Thing as an Accident of the Spirit," "Seven Years Sober," "Ghazal for a National Emergency"
The Paris Review: "Mothers I Once Was," "An Oversight," "Famous Americans and Why They Were Wrong"
Peripheries: "Ghazal for the Men I Once Was," "The Miracle," "Pilgrim Bell (I demand)," "In the Language of Mammon"
Ploughshares: "There Are 7,000 Living Languages," "Pilgrim Bell (The self I am today)"
Poetry: "Despite My Efforts Even My Prayers Have Turned into Threats," "Forfeiting My Mystique," "Pilgrim Bell (How long can you speak)," "Vines"
The Rumpus: "Shadian Incident"
Tin House: "I Wouldn't Even Know What to Do with a Third Chance"
The Virginia Quarterly Review: "Reza's Restaurant, Chicago, 1997," "Pilgrim Bell (The stillness you prize)," "Escape to the Palace"

Several of these poems first appeared in the limited-edition chapbooks *Team Mashallah* and *Team Mashallah II*, co-authored with Hanif Abdurraqib, Fatimah Asghar, Safia Elhillo, and Angel Nafis.

"Reza's Restaurant, Chicago, 1997" was reprinted in the 2020 *Pushcart Prize Anthology*.

Reader, thank you.

Hanif Abdurraqib, Hannah Aizenman, Kazim Ali, Debra Allbery, Eloisa Amezcua, Kasey Anderson, Fatimah Asghar, Zain Aslam, Hannah Bagshaw, Noah Baldino, Dan Barden, Ruth Baumann, Chase Berggrun, Frank Bidart, Maria Bedford, Marianne Boruch, Gabrielle Calvocoressi, Jos Charles, Cortney Lamar Charleston, Heather Christle, Franny Choi, Eduardo C. Corral, Christopher DeWeese, Natalie Diaz, Gary Dop, Camille Dungy, Carolina Ebeid, Shira Erlichman, Safia Elhillo, Andrew Epstein, Katie Farris, Chris Forhan, Christopher Gaumer, francine j. harris, Steve Henn, Jane Hirshfield, Mira Jacob, Leslie Jamison, Kamran Javadizadeh, Ilya Kaminsky, Mary Karr, Vivian Lee, Zach Linge, Jennifer Loyd, Layli Long Soldier, Daschielle Louis, Nabila Lovelace, Alessandra Lynch, Nate Marshall, Angel Nafis, Hieu Minh Nguyen, José Olivarez, Matthew Olzmann, Tommy Orange, Don Platt, Ben Purkert, Mike Purol, Megan Denton Ray, Jayme Ringleb, sam sax, Claire Schwartz, Don Share, Solmaz Sharif, Marisa Siegel, Clint Smith, Danez Smith, David J. Thompson, Bradley Trumpfheller, Jack Underwood, R.A. Villanueva, G.C. Waldrep, Phillip B. Williams, Kevin Young: these poems and I are better made for having spent time with you. Thank you.

To the Lannan and Ragdale Foundations: thank you. To my students and colleagues at Purdue, Randolph, and Warren Wilson: thank you. Alba Ziegler-Bailey, Jacqueline Ko, Sarah Chalfant: thank you. Parisa Ebrahimi, Chantz Erolin, Fiona McCrae: thank you. Marisa Atkinson, Katie Dublinski, Caroline Nitz, Casey O'Neil, thank you. Tabia Yapp, I'm grateful for you every day. Thank you. Jeff Shotts, the visionary. Our oracle. Thank you. Mammy, Wanda, Mytoan, Arash, Layla, Nora: thank you. Paige Lewis, the total noun. Thank you. You are in every line.

KAVEH AKBAR is the author of a previous poetry collection, *Calling a Wolf a Wolf,* and editor of *The Penguin Book of Spiritual Verse.* His poems have appeared in the *New Yorker,* the *New York Times,* the *Paris Review,* and in *The Best American Poetry.* Born in Tehran, Iran, Akbar teaches at Purdue University and in the low-residency MFA programs at Randolph College and Warren Wilson. He serves as the poetry editor of the *Nation.*

The text of *Pilgrim Bell* is set in Arno Pro.
Book design by Rachel Holscher.
Composition by Bookmobile Design & Digital
Publisher Services, Minneapolis, Minnesota.
Manufactured by McNaughton & Gunn on acid-free,
100 percent postconsumer wastepaper